Vendettas, Charms, and Prayers

WITHDRAWN

# Vendettas, Charms, and Prayers

*Poems by*
## PAMELA GEMIN

Minnesota Voices Project Number 91
NEW RIVERS PRESS 1999

First edition
Library of Congress Card Catalog Number: 98-89713
ISBN: 0-89823-195-7
Edited by John Reinhard
Book design and typesetting by MacLean and Tuminelly
This book was typeset using Fontshop Scala and Scala Sans typefaces, with display type
set in SpillMilk Regular by FontHead Design
Printed in Canada

NEW RIVERS PRESS is a nonprofit literary press dedicated to publishing the very best
emerging writers in our region, nation, and world.

The publication of *Vendettas, Charms, and Prayers* has been made possible by generous
grants from the Jerome Foundation; the North Dakota Council on the Arts; and Dayton
Hudson Foundation on behalf of Dayton's, Mervyn's California, and Target Stores.

Additional support has been provided by the General Mills Foundation, the McKnight
Foundation, the Star Tribune Foundation, and the contributing members of New Rivers
Press.

NATIONAL ENDOWMENT FOR THE ARTS

MINNESOTA STATE ARTS BOARD

NORTH DAKOTA COUNCIL ON THE ARTS

New Rivers Press
420 North Fifth Street
Minneapolis, MN 55401

www.mtn.org/newrivpr

This book is for my father, who taught me to love language;
and my mother, who let me find my own;
and my husband, Joseph, without whom . . .

# Acknowledgments

Thanks to the following publications, where many of these poems first appeared, sometimes in earlier versions:

*Bakunin:* "Confirmation Day"

*Bellowing Ark:* "Aurora, July Downhill" and "The Knots"

*Blue Moon Review:* "Me & River Phoenix," "The 3:15," "Senior Picture, 1971," "Vandal," and "Washing the Darlings"

*Calyx:* "Birth Control"

*Encodings:* "Professor Love"

*Farmer's Market:* "Almost Winter" and "The Crow Shooter"

*Great River Review:* "The Borrowed House"

*Green Mountains Review Special Issue: American Poetry at the End of the Millennium:* "When Van Morrison Sang"

*Hurricane Alice:* "Toyland" and "When She Went"

*Madison Review:* "X-Ray Tech"

*New Delta Review:* "Bombshelter"

*North Coast Review:* "Lifejackets"

*Passages North:* "Aurora, July Woods"

*Patterns:* "To the Doe Last Seen"

*Phoebe:* "Down There"

*Primavera:* "Cleanup," "Drinking Song," "Eve, Seeing Red," "Fourth of July," "Upper Peninsula Landscape with Aunts," and "The Visible Man"

*South Dakota Review:* "Roberta"

*Spoon River Poetry Review:* "Down to God's," "Enemy Mine," "Flashback, 1973," and "That Woman"

*Wisconsin Academy Review:* "Stealing Lilacs"

"Aurora, July Downhill" also appears in the anthology
*Family: A Celebration*, published by Peterson's Press, 1995.

"Senior Picture, 1971" and "When Van Morrison Sang" also appear in
*Boomer Girls: Poems by Women from the Baby Boom Generation*, published
by the University of Iowa Press in 1999.

For their early encouragement, thanks to Dr. Eugene Haun and Dr.
Nadean Bishop, first mentors. For their generous help with this book
through its thousand incarnations, thanks to David ("Lit Boy") Graham,
Julie King, Jef Leisgang, Paula Sergi, and Kate Sontag. For decades of
friendship and wisdom, thanks to Kim Edwards, Janet Norton, Ellen
Shriner, Rich Rummel, Sue Rummel, Judy Vilmain, and the Fabulous Port
Huron Girls: Julie, Joan, and Gail. For their generous doses of daily faith,
thanks to Dr. Estella Lauter and my colleagues at UW Oshkosh, especially
Charlie, Doug, Jane, Kathleen, Kay, Karl, Marguerite, P. K., Paul, Ron, and
Sandy. For their steadfast editorial support, thanks to Ruth Young and her
coeditors at *Primavera* magazine; and for the great gifts of space, time,
prairie walks, and home cooking, thanks to the Ragdale Foundation in
Lake Forest, Illinois, where this manuscript was completed. A very special
thanks to John Reinhard, my friend and Editor Extraordinaire: *long may
you run*.

# Contents

## THREE   That Woman

## FOUR   Toyland

# ONE

# The Knots

# The 3:15

Not from the wrong side of,
but right on the tracks,
from the storybook land
of the Boxcar Children,
buttercups, milkweed leaning
down long slopes of grass
from our yard to rails and ties.

Not poor, never poor, not wanting
for meat or fruit, for light or heat,
but burning the way
we Americans burn, climbing
each slippery rung of the beanstalk
up to a well-feathered nest, a golden egg.

I grew up thinking *goddamn*
was a color, a brand
we'd been sucker-sold and stuck with,
grew up believing
that all our appliances bled.

The neighbors had Buicks or Fords
and my dad had a Goddamn Car,
the goddamn lawn to mow,
the bloody washing machine on the blink,
the goddamn woodpeckers up on the roof
on Saturday morning, pecking away
on the TV antenna
the one goddamn time
he wasn't ripped out of bed
at the crack of dawn.

When she just couldn't stand it herself,
my mom said "G.D." – "Get back in this G.D. house
and drink your milk!" And I said "dod damn,"
as in "Dimmee a dod damn cookie, please," or
"Here come that dod damn train again,"
as the rusty CN and Chesapeake boxcars

blasted on by, rattling the spoons
inside of our drawers,
making the peeling panes hum.

And later, when it roared back
in the belly of night, that train
rocked us all awake to kick off
warm blankets or tuck them
more tightly around each other,
then rocked us back to dreamland
with clack-chukka rhythms,
the bums in red boxcars asleep
in its clattering song:

3:15 A.M. and all is well
on the dead end of 9th Street, all's well
in the USA, in the goddamn world.

# Confirmation Day

O Bernadette, the day I took your name,
I woke with berry rashes on my palms
and clappers clanging in my ears;
I'd dreamt the heart of Jesus,
full of thorns and pickers,
was wrapped in butcher's paper
in the kitchen cupboard,
leaking but still beating
among Oreos and Pop Tarts,
thump thump thumping with a message
just for me.

O Bernadette, the day I took your name,
my hair was done in pincurls, one by one,
and rounded bangs.
My stiff little dress crunched into the pew,
my scabby knees mashed on the kneeler,
but after this I'd get a half a dozen
holy laminations, dollar-bill cards from all of my aunts,
your name to keep forever,
and a large cherry Coke from Woolworth's.

O Bernadette, I saw us, you and me
down at that dime store fountain,
sharing an icy cold Coke with two straws,
splitting an order of golden fries,
sketching some possible nicknames
on napkins (Bernie? Nadie? Dettie?)
or shopping for 45's and then catching an Elvis
down at the Huron, stopping on our way home
by the bridge DQ for a Mr. Misty.
You'll like this town.

I want you to sleep over tonight and every night;
I want to set your hair in big brush rollers,
rat it when it's dry,
then spray it with Aqua Net,

higher and higher and higher.
Some dangly earrings,
some Maybelline blue,
some lip gloss and liner
and all the boys will know
what the Four Tops are talking about.

Bernadette, you're the soul of me.
My princess of heartbeats,
my name-saint, my best girlfriend.
Please don't go back to France.
We could have such a blast.

# Washing the Darlings

Mornings he wasn't crocked on Ripple,
old man Darling, toothless and fourteen times
as mean as my old man,
hauled navy beans from trucks
to freighter docks, his back bent bearing
hundred-pound bean sacks,
sad radio songs of runaway wives, and the brunt
of being left with seven children, six boys
and a single girl.

They filled their pants and sat;
they picked their noses.
Wild cootie bugs jumped in their undies,
those Darling boys.
They were *out of control;*
at the center of every grade school storm
at South Park School, you'd find
at least one Darling
slugging it out in those famous
flagpole fights unfurling
under the Wolverine State banner,
under the red white and blue,
their chubby fists pounding,
their raggedy dirt-caked nails
slicing little red half-moon marks
into tormentors' flesh.

No sin to be poor, my aunt June said,
in the old days we all were poor,
but we were *clean.* How much could it cost
for the old man to keep his kids clean?
Uncle Ty, volunteer fireman, said
he'd like to hose them Darlings down,
just take and pressure blast 'em all,
but what about the girl, I said, Diana,
I want her.

Diana, the first time I saw you,
hunched into that corner
of Mrs. Maxwell's class,
scratching the bites on your stubby arms,
picking at lace on your stained anklets,
I wanted to kidnap you, carry you home
to soak and soak in our steamy clawfoot tub
till the filth surrendered
to gardenia bubbles, lather its layers
off with the softest sponge;

then tilt your head back
and welcome you in
to the emerald city of Prell,
a shampoo so luxurious
pearls swam in its woman-shaped bottles
on TV.

Later we'd coax your hair
from its mousy bowlcut,
finger wave spitcurls,
paint your nails Peony Frost.
Later we'd dip our pinkies
into Aunt June's stash
of Evening in Paris,
scent your white wrists, your white nape,
your fresh sun-dried bloomers,
get you spiffed.

But first we'd have to wrap you
head to toe in soft white terry cloth,
scour off the final ring of insult
from the porcelain, and rinse
and rinse
and rinse
till the water came sparkling.

# Down to God's

On Sundays, we never said
"Let's go to God's place," the way
we'd go down to Aunt Dot's
or Aunt Ruthie's, but still
where He hung His great Stetson,
kicked off His gigantic sandals,
felt just like home sometimes
with the light pounding down
through diamonds of jewel-tone windows, the rise
of my uncles' eyebrows in Latin chants,
and the cool swish, swish of the handsome
young Father Dlugi's robes
as he sidestepped shyly
along the Communion rail, trace
of his wonderful aftershave
still sweet upon his fingers as he
fed us the body of Christ, amen.
The gals down to God's
were spitcurled and sprayed in place
and dressed to break commandments;
mahogany pews oiled so slick
the boys could slide, pink marble sills
so smooth and cool you could lie down
and sleep for a hundred years, and oh the fat
white candles He'd have lit
for dead grandmas and grandpas and all
the Holy Rollers. Wouldn't you love
to have a place like that someday
when we make it big,
is what everyone must have said
as they buckled themselves
into Ramblers and Falcons
and headed to the Honeybee for breakfast,
down the wide streets from God's.

# Flashback, 1973

When the car breaks down
in the wrung-out end of summer,
I take the downtown bus
to Walgreen's for the must-have-nows
of my life: orange juice, coffee,
birth control pills.

When the bus door pumps open
it's twenty years ago; I'm nineteen,
the last virgin in Fort Lauderdale,
on my way to the free clinic,
sweat-covered bus fare dime in my hand,
lump of homesickness tight in my throat;

but I'm going to do it, get the pills
before my boyfriend comes
down from Wisconsin next month;
I'm going to give him what he wants,
be glad to be rid of it, really,
the weight, the pain of its preciousness,
he can have it.

In the line that stretches out
to the sidewalk, I stand under palms
with runaways, prostitutes, other
poor girls and women, unashamed
until the doctor has me naked,
stirrup-ready, speculum-ready
between his paper sheets,
asks why I want the pills,
laughs out loud when I tell him my plan,

hands me a sample pack of 1-80s, says
*Just ask your girlfriends
how to take these*, winks and yells
*NEXT!* as he shows me to the door.

Three weeks later I'm childproofed but drowning
in my body's water, eyelids swollen shut,
fingers fat sewn-together sausages,
stung-looking lips, and any day now
the boy will get off the plane,

the boy I love,
am certain I will die loving;
but he will not be the one
I give it to after all,
the Cracker Jack prize you can't tape back,

and he'll hate me for that,
grind it between his teeth at night
long after he's married somebody else
and left me to hear it
in line at the movies,

and I will bounce again
on the hard blue plastic
seat of that hurt
all the way downtown.

# Me & River Phoenix

*Whatever was bound to happen*
*in my story did not happen.*
    — Lisel Mueller, "In November"

When me & River
go down to the mall,
he steers me past racks
of crushed velvet skullcaps,
laced-piped magenta leggings,
leather-thong pendants tied
with peace signs & ankhs.

His own skinny knees
popping out of his jeans,
he elbows me up escalators
where ladies' wrinkle-free knits
& cardigans hang
in their solid neutrality:
English teacher clothes.

Yet when we're in the record store,
he looks down his nose
when I stock up on R&B classics,
implores me to give Blind/Smashing/
Screaming/Lemon/Melon/
Pumpkinheads a chance;

& when me & River
do lunch in the food court,
he scolds me for scarfing
the tacos & dairy dessert I bought
just to watch him roll his eyes.

In the flickering dark
of the cineplex,
as I search for any hope of profile
under those lank strings of hair
he keeps shaking back,

I can't decide whether
I want to kiss him, full
on the mouth, or whomp him & his whole
generation of snotty ingrates
a good one upside their head.

That is, until he dies.
Face down in the pool of my twenties,
stagnant with warming beer & the floating
butts of Kool King Menthols, floating pieces
of my busted-up heart,
dies from all the times
I drove home loaded, one eye shut,
crazy to party some more.

Then I take him as my brother.
Then I rise up in his name
& keep rolling on.

# Jennifer's Reason

Their reasons are always just notes
in the same old top 40 hit:
dead grandmothers, cars and computers and cats,
bladder and sinus infections, hangovers,
crisis-driven love, and frankly sometimes
I just don't care; I don't want to know
the reason they couldn't be here, in class
with the rest of us; tell you the truth
sometimes I'm only pretending
to listen, nodding and frowning
those tight-lipped teacher frowns
that say *Junior, forget it.*

Their reasons walk with us
from class to class; we laugh
to each other at coffee: their poses,
their tiny tight lives and enormous pants,
the multiple holes in their noses and navels,
their incredulous tie-dyed hair
that's supposed to say – what? and to whom?
and their backwards baseball caps, the unbearable
clatter and thump they call their music.

> Oh you wouldn't believe
> what one told me today –
> that *Citizen Kane* was not
> about Hearst after all,
> and he has *proof!*

> Oh you wouldn't believe
> the shallow small-town
> mentality of these kids,
> their naïveté –
> they can't write
> a sentence in English
> and they think they're gonna be *lawyers!*

Oh you wouldn't believe
this willow reed flute of a blonde
with buzz-cut hair,
this Jenni Somebody,
who couldn't look up
through her navy blue lashes
to tell me the reason
her poem wasn't ready for class today,
the reason she couldn't be there.

Nineteen or twenty, navy blue smears
from eyes to cheeks to chin, she says
she was in the psych ward again.
*But I didn't OD this time,* she tells me,
*My boyfriend tried to kill me.*

Jenni's excuse is so bright when it falls
it explodes into stars, into bullets
and fire shards shooting
out over our heads
and just then there is nothing
I would not do for this girl, no money
or lie too big to spend.

Her reason walks with me
for days and days; I'd send locusts
and skulls to her enemy's doorstep,
buy her breakfast, even write her poem.

# When Van Morrison Sang

"Tupelo Honey,"
wouldn't we all turn to satin inside,
we girls playing euchre
and smoking and tossing back
lipsticked longnecks, hips rocking
out of our chairs
those Friday nights at Donna's?

She was already divorced by then,
but weren't we all still such believers;
didn't we close our eyes
and scream Jesus, I *love* this song,
even with Donna's heart
pounded flat, chicken-fried and forked up
on a Melmac platter; oh

hadn't we been through that blender
one speed or another;
hadn't we lived to tell
it again, threading it in
and out of Friday nights when Van
went down the hatch
all ginger smoke and sweetness?

And yes, we all wanted good jobs
for fair money, and cars
that would make it home,
and each other's lifetime love,
but sometimes, if only for Friday night,
didn't we just want to be
that girl

Van Morrison sang about,
that "angel of the first degree,"
who could ruffle her wings,
pass her glittering wand
over Van and his kind,
and make such music,
make a man sing like that?

# Enemy Mine

*I put a spell on you / because you're mine . . .*
    — Screamin' Jay Hawkins

No enemies, not one
since Connie Pendergrast,
who spread it all downtown
I gave under-the-sweaters,
said I stole Kenny Ammerman off her porch
and took him down under the bridge
to Canada, got pink mohair fuzz
all over him, collar to socks.

For months I rubbed
her lies on me,
carried their strange perfume
behind my ears,
picked at the rash
of her nastiness.

By the tenth class reunion
she still hadn't gotten her breasts,
that Connie, hair still pale
and poker straight, hacked into
that same dirty shag.
Hooked up with some dim wrestler,
runs in her nylons, drunk,
ass melting to blubber,
still working at Farmer Jack's.
It made me happy.

None since Connie Pendergrast,
no enemy but you, grown woman
whose shadow I swam in,
whose lies I peel off me now
like water weeds,
whose motherly bosom
hides an eighth-grade heart.

Me and you girl,
after school, out by the flagpole.
*Say your prayers.*
I'm going to rip your bra straps,

shred your new skirt,
throw your new shoes in the road.
Yank hunks of your silvering hair out,
flecks of burning scalp
still clinging to each root.

Or be chamomile-sweet a year from now,
when we meet at the sink
in the women's john during some intermission,
you out on the town
the first time since your breakdown.

Under your eyes, in cruel blue florescence,
a crisscross of brand new lines
and baby red spiders asleep
in the saggy pouches of your face.

It's made you old
and sick and tired,
this business of betrayal.
And that makes me happy.

# The Knots

I learned about patience
sitting in women's laps, listening
to the soft *pop* of thread
drawn in, drawn out of linen
stretched taut on women's hoops,
waiting for leaves and flowers
to make themselves known.

By college I knew the fancy stitches,
took orders in dorms, satin-stitched palms
and ocean waves on the backs
of denim work shirts,
split women's old jean seams
out to skirts, embroidered the smiling sun,
the moon and stars in gold and silver sequins,
tacked on shells and beads.

Years later, stuck
in a prairie town winter,
I tried it again, did cross-stitch
to keep from smoking,
to cultivate a hobby
requiring sobriety.
This time I bought myself pattern books,
plotted out runners and throws
and guest towels (I had no guests),
went mad in the name of microscopic x's.

But one night after happy hour
they all came back into my hands:
the backstitch, whipped-chain, french knot,
feather, fishbone, seed, and fly,
the lazy daisy, back
like crazy old friends;
and I welcomed them all
in a frenzy of color, stayed up all night

embroidering wild samplers
on ripe white sheets.

Of course underneath it's a mess
of mottled tangles,
a stitch-ripper's nightmare.
I did it too fast, like everything else,
got reckless, abandoned my plan,
made up as I went.

But still, it almost looks
as if I knew what I was doing;
as if maybe, if I hadn't told you
about the knots,
you'd never have known.

# TWO

# Lifejackets

# Roberta

Roberta, girl cousin,
the stalks are ready in their green rows.
Between them we once bent in hiding,
fists in our mouths,
while our mothers
called us to supper.

Remember Menominee, fast and black,
the old tree bent over it,
crayfish and boys
crawling on red sand.

With long branches we walked the cows
down from the clearing
smoking stolen cigarettes,
covering our breath
with wild chives.

Roberta, we are twenty-four tonight
and still smoking,
here on the porch of your new house.
July gives us our annual togetherness,
pulls me up from my place on the map
and sets me down here,
where we learned to be girls together.

Your baby boy is ready for walking.
He giggles in his crib.
Your gambling husband
has left you again;
your plumbing has chosen
this evening to undo itself
and he has taken the tools.

Cousin, I would tell you
how I've thrown away
another good man,
if only the northern lights

had not appeared, just now,
and the wind had not shifted
so suddenly against us,
and I had not remembered
what the older ones,
the aunts and the mothers,
will tell us forever:
that we will be women soon enough
and not to worry,
to just be girls.

# Man's Man

*To Ron Rindo*

I know where I can find you,
deep in the tavern poker game,
winning again, dragging your Viceroy,
rattling ice in your highball glass,
just enough pleased with yourself,
the best looking man in the bar,
in the town of Ishpeming – hell,
in the whole damn peninsula.

Cousin Jack Cornish miner's son,
drinking man, barroom brawling man,
every woman's pitter-patter
mercy-here-he-comes man,
six feet of lean hooked up
to Hollywood shoulders,
black hair in thick waves,
black eyes they said came through town
on a gypsy wagon;
don't even get me started on your smile.

Coming up behind you I smell cedar
so strong the smoke and Old Spice
don't stand a chance, and jackpine,
the woodsmell that never came off
your hands, your caps, your hunting jacket,
cedar-and-pine-smelling last of the Michigan woodsmen
I followed through ferns to where sugarplums grew,
snagging my hair on thorns, pulling
gooseberry pickers and burrs
from my pantlegs;

and now I've come out of the woods to tell you,
banged through these swinging doors of my dreams
to tell you I've never stopped following, grandfather;
still running after your scent

and tracking the print of your boot
stamped onto every man I've wanted,

and today you're twice as dangerous to love.
Well-marbled beef and bacon man,
butter-soaked biscuit and gravy man,
second slab à la mode pie, black coffee,
shot-tossing, straight-up-and-sweetheart-
leave-the-bottle man,

I'm right behind you and your five o'clock shadow;
man who can't stay put with one good woman,
can't say no to one too many,
can't do without that gun in his glove compartment.
Man with his red flannel shirtpockets
full of hickory nuts, chipmunks
running up and down his legs, his trunk,
the branches of his arms.

# Aurora, July Woods

Little town of trillium and hay,
of straight corn rows, ripe peas
and raspberries,
place of things ever being picked
and washed clean
and eaten from stone bowls.

This summer you are kinder
than you have ever been,
tender with tall copper rocks,
steep red bluffs, deep trees;

and I should be a ruby-throated hummingbird,
should hover over you from higher air.
Instead I'm a city girl
faking my way through your woods,
daring to turn my eyes
toward a rustle in the ferns.

My mother must have hid herself here once,
from her five sisters, and spun
a secret thought of me.
For us there have been wordless
knots and untyings.
These same woods that were her walls
are now my open places.

Here she must have listened
for someone on his way to her
and raised up her face
like a flower;
the scent of it still everywhere,
the shiver,
the long breath of design.

# The Crow Shooter

Because he despises their squawking, hell-sent selves
descending on blue-black wings in noonday sun,

he wants to see crows' blood pump out of buckshot holes
to spill upon his fences; wants to see their eyes of coal

cloud over, halt their warnings in mid-scream, stop the cawing
mockery and laughter, and the motion of chiseling beaks

made for picking his big blue eyes out. He promises daughters
crowbird pies, blackfeather pillow stuffing,

but they know who their father is, know what he hates about crows
is really those featherboned wings that take crows

where their father can't go; and the way they will always
come back again glistening, dodging his bullets

if that's what it takes, to do what they came to do,
work ornery tendons away from bones, pick

and peck till sockets are polished clean of flesh, their satin
heads nodding yes; and the way they'll risk everything.

# Drinking Song

You know it from way back, don't you?
Its secret chords.
When you were a boy
your momma could sweep

her sleepy-eyed brood
lickety split down the stairs
with your pillows, the babies
still sucking their thumbs,

and lock you all
in the old sedan big as a house,
sing lullaby prayers
to her good children

up and down the county trunks
all night long.
In patches of your bumpity sleep
you saw your hazy daddy

stumble through the bean rows,
heard your name
in his throaty cough.
You knew that smell

of his whiskery kiss
as well as you knew
his pockets would be full
of caramels

in the morning,
as well as you knew
you'd come home
to his whippoorwill whistle.

After the war
your purple heart brother
came up the driveway drunk
and stayed that way;

drunk the night he crept
from bed to bed
to round the family up; drunk

with the orders he gave you all
to march,
hands behind your heads,
to the basement to hide
from the Cong; drunk
when he swore he'd shoot you all,
if that's what it came to,
before he gave up
the position.

When he died in a cabin as smoky
as any tavern, not forty years old,
nobody could understand it:
all he'd ever drunk was beer.

You married what you knew,
a girl whose people drank;
her legends of knocked-over Christmas trees
and black-eyed birthday brawls

made sense; her words
cut mean as razor wire;
she made a mean child whose words
cut mean as razor wire.

You watched as drink pickled
all their heads, pickled
all of their hearts-on-a-stick,
but never tasted.

Under your breath
you sang the song
you knew by heart,
swept up

their broken dish messes,
kept sewing them all
back together
seamless, singing.

# Lifejackets

Tied into their chilly embrace
we could only look straight ahead,
but they did their job,

kept us bobbing afloat,
fallen from skis or drifted
out over our heads; preserved us

like guardian saints
from dark currents
and lilypad tangles; kept us above

the bottomless green-black muck
of that wild lake
that took our cousin.

We who came back after that
wore bright red vests
and were counted out loud.

When we dog-paddled onto the rocks
Aunt June undid the triple knots
and peeled them off us,

called us her *waterbugs*, speckled
and chilled, folded us
into clean towels and rubbed us dry.

And when they were finished
saving our lives, they hung
by their strings on clothespins

behind the trailer,
lines of soggy lobsters
tied and kicking between birches,

caught in the smoke of roasting corn,
those jackets
that never dried through.

# To the Doe Last Seen
## Running Up the South Exit Ramp
## toward Wal*Mart Plaza

Through rearview mirrors
you promise her
the worst is almost over:
fur bristling, ears prickling,
horns honking,
clack of her scattering hooves
on asphalt, delicate lungs
pumped full of diesel exhaust.
In her blown-glass eyes
you read the history of prey,
whole chapters cut loose and let fly
over cloverleaf roads,
pages tearing in the whizzing force
of arrows, bullets, engines.
She's already the star
of somebody's coffee room story.
By lunchtime
she will have been somebody's reason
to kiss and make up,
go back to church,
to reconsider everything;
somebody's chance to breathe deep,
let the last, best breath
of wildness run out in a whistle,
stroking the dented fender
or brushing the scrape
of blue paint from her tail.
And if you weren't already
late for work,
if you could take
just one wild ride again

you'd take it now,
in the wisps
of her velveteen ears,
be the whisper that tells her
    Wait
        Steady
           Now
              Go
                  *Run*

# Stealing Lilacs

Long before the arboretum opens,
I wake with that scent
already on my breath,

steal off
with my kitchen shears
already drunk on the promise

of green bushes bent
with the deep grape weight of them;
hungover with ivory pink

clusters hanging like moonlight;
globes of split flutes
peeling out in their namesake hue,

that creamy blue edible violet
spread across branches: understand,
I'm here to take your lilacs.

Last night I sang
to the firecracker planet Mars,
to Jupiter rising above the garage,

danced in my nightgown
out in the driveway
just before midnight,

barefoot, whirling,
breathing in late May visions
of creamy blue deep grape ivory pink

bunches of lilacs cut loose
and fresh, and quenching themselves
in every available vase

on every ledge, shelf, sill, and mantel;
lilacs sent up and down stairs
in bottles and bowls;

set gaily afloat in shoes
and sinks; in tubs and tanks,
strewn upon pillows,

tucked between sheets, between teeth,
between legs, behind ears,
under noses and arms;

and yes I know
you have to lock me up
but bring me lilacs.

# The Borrowed House

This isn't our table, that wasn't our bed,
the garden with its brittle vines not ours.

This isn't my window; I break the house rules
smoking and brushing my hair in the kitchen,

one room inside one house so far inside
this blooming prairie, nobody I long for

could ever find me here. An afternoon of sherry
has gone down in shades of green. The wind

has hung new seedlings in the screens,
and nothing has happened here for a hundred years.

The rage of that sameness stuck into the walls
where the calendars hang, surprised.

Those stories are true, of ropes strung house to barn
in winter, of women snapped wild when the world

would not move from the doorway, endless miles
of white or green or brittle brown, the same;

and the tale of a man found frozen, eyes still open, half in
and half out of a window frame, his mittens and keys

gone lost in the snow. Something in this room has always
waited to go wrong. If I shift in my chair, the curtains will fly

into flames. Pink bowls will explode in the cupboards.
Those shelves of bright things will come down

and be heard from: peaches, pears, and apricots,
vendettas, charms, and prayers.

# Almost Winter

Just now, when ice first cuts
its little teeth in doorways,
now I remember your name.

When I breathe in and out
your name takes a vapor, its shape
rising warm when I say it.

When my leather sleeves crunch stiff,
when it's hot buttered rum or snifters
of liqueur I hit the streets for,

your name is the storm
under my hat, snow-ghost,
guest in my day who will stay me,

running through my ears
in strings of bass notes,
beats of nearby drums.

*Come on, come on, come back,*
they call. Tear up the map;
tonight we march by the stars!

These almost winter mornings
the moon stays home.
As you wake with your love

in the mountains of other countries,
I conjure your voice, your collar,
your black hair in streetlight; your name

seeping out of the distance,
fresh snow on the river,
frost on the lawn.

# Aurora, July Downhill

Fresh from a rainstorm
I walk the hill down
from Aunt Dorothy's, down
this narrow road I know by heart,
bordered by purple milkweed,
fern fronds, fool's oats, pincherry trees,
and the buttercup wands we waved
under our cousins' chins.

Downhill, past my great aunt's
house and garden, cooler than October here
July's last night; chilly under muslin,
feet cold in summer sandals,
under them this road, the stony
lumps of it stuck in the tar like toads.

Downhill, past the *bobwire* fence
stretched open on the path to Carlsen's crick.
Fence of rusty metal thorns
(the better to infect you),
of backs bent over sideways,
slashed ankles, bleeding palms.

And all for a brook trout
dipped in flour, real butter-fried,
to suffer the feel of the doomed
red worm on your hook;
that flash of fighting colors
when the fish bit,
silver belly puffing in and out;
the look in her eye you took with you;
the tickle of her thin bones
no cough could cure.

Down past the maples
that shaded our horses,
down past the stream
still clear enough to read through,

down past the barn and haybed,
down past the jagged copper bluff
we climbed to scribble our true loves' names.

Down past the riverbank muck, straight down,
where toeprints must be fossilized somewhere.
The swipe of our muddy feet
as we ran up momentum, the push, the jump,
the sting of hair on eyelids,
the burn of the rope in our hands
as we swung out over the snake-black water,
screaming.

My Grandma Sara and all of her daughters,
all the O'Riley girls,
lugged gallons of hand-filled ravioli
under these willows, and racks of homemade pasties,
hundred-pound honey-glazed hams;
dozens of French Canadian pork pies,
tins and tins of bars, bars, butterscotch,
coconut, chocolate chip, cherry-cheese,
apricot, oatmeal, nutmeg –
then they said we all should *have some more* . . .

Those days the men played cards
on picnic tables, smoking,
bare-chested, lean-muscled, young,
unshaven on their day off,
children on their laps
and happy with beer.

Before my cousin Kenny
    drowned in the lake;
before my cousin Nicky
    died of meningitis;
before my grandpas' hearts gave out
    or Uncle Frank drove into that wall;
before cancer moved into Aunt June

and Aunt June moved out,
    or I lost my Grandma Sara
    (first to the TV preachers
    and then again
    when her kidneys quit).
Before Lee Ann's divorce,
    or Rosalie's, or Little Sara's;
before Uncle Benny's strokes,
    when they still said he drank
    on account of The War;
before any of us knew
    those secrets we dug so relentlessly for
    would rush up from the caverns
    to scald us blind,

this is the place we lay in dozens,
cool-skinned and damp-haired,
fresh from the river,
dozing together, hard little bellies full,
in perfect safety.

Now thirty years gone,
as simply and much
as sun and rain, I'm still welcome
all down this hill.
And everything around me bows deeply,
steps aside,
to make room.

THREE

# That Woman

# Eve, Seeing Red

When we squat in our circles
in front of the fire, our green
pleats, the tents of our skirts
just inches off earth;

when we click-clack
with tongues, call out
to our blood, the tents
of our skirts

just inches off iron-shot earth,
nobody has to say scarlet,
maroon, cerise: we see it
coming, eyes open or closed.

When Eve bit the red fruit
she swallowed the core, I
swallowed the core, we all
swallowed the core;

and the sharp yellow husk, its seed
cradle shaped like a star,
cut tracks in the roof
of her mouth; and the little

black jacket skin of the seed
went down into her round belly
and fell away, and now
there are orchards

shot up in the damp
red sponges of lungs;
and now the white blossoms
are raining in rows;

and now the green fruit
moves ripe and all ladders
lead up to red lands;
and now the empty pails

will sing and sing. What else
was He thinking
to push those awful teeth
into her red gums?

# Birth Control

To the daughters and sons
I have never let be,
those eggs arrested monthly,
those furious paddling seeds surprised,
my apologies slosh
in the hem of my skin,
spiny animals in a stew.

You have witnessed shells breaking
under the sheer will of pearls,
felt the terrible pull of moons,
whispered your names in the ears
of impossible fathers, postponed yourselves
further and further.

You may come to be only
long looks backwards,
empty needles, pools of sighs,
and still you are as faithful
as steam rising from the face of a lake,
as constant and polite as steeping tea.

Simmering children, waiting like snails,
you are the traps love leaves
cocked in the shadows,
the only hope left of a name.

# Those Bayes Girls

    gleamed, like ultra brite choppers
zapped blue-white
by a TV wand,
    dazzled all the boys witless,
squinting in their high beams,
their minty fresh breath,
their perfect bangs,
their Bonnie Doon kneesocks
rolled down once
beneath their hairless knees.

All of our moms said:
    Melissa Bayes
would never tease
or layer
or dye her *hair!*
    Melody Bayes
would never
be caught dead
*smoking!*
    Marianne Bayes
would never
come home *drunk!*

Those Bayes girls
didn't have dark sides, so
they married dark-sided men
who stained sheets and driveways
and bath tiles and jungle floors
with men's dark blood,

and the Bayes girls,
    Melissa
    Melody
    Marianne,
emptied their pale blue
nightgowns upon them,
fit peppermint lips
to men's dark mouths,

emptied men's dark caves
of pain and filled them
with ice blue stars.

# That Woman

Just as you imagined, she has silk
and cream for skin and sleeps naked.

Hazelnut chocolate from cut glass bowls
flavors the tips of her tapered nails,

melts in her coral mouth. As you walk
through the soft amber light of her rooms,

after the scent of her hair, you know this comfort
could be dangerous: real butter there

and still-warm loaves, the stovelight glowing.
Open palms across the lace-topped table,

no children to leave stains. It could be your grandma's
if not for the thrill of sin; it could be heaven.

That woman knows your code, upside down and backwards,
is fluent in all of your long lost tongues.

*I know,* she says, *tell me everything. I have no plans
for the evening,* the weekend, the holidays, the next ten years.

But we all know what happens now: you leave
and she keeps fading, light prints in steam.

Some days you might wake to a trace of a scent of lilacs,
a whiff of curry simmering, or taste her again

in a flavor like nutmeg, swear you hear her name in violins.
Meanwhile, she goes on, of course, doing what she knows.

Born to recline on dimpled hips, her soft dry hands
working knots from the next man's muscles,

under her breast the weight of the diehard
concubine, the heavy heart of gold.

# When She Went

She'd long gone strange;
a yellowed button
stuck on a cuff,
an odd bead slid back
to the clasp;
strange and mean for business
like the bristle broom some swore
they'd seen her bump across the sky on,
but not much later
too simple to leave the yard.
Shocks of white quills
shooting up from her skull,
bird eyes at ends
of tunnels, moles
on her low-slung nose,
lips inside out.
*What the hell youse kids want?*
was the question she sent
through the fence slats,
*Who the world are youse people?*
When she finally went
we shone flashlights
under her porch,
looked for rubies in flowerpots,
silver certificates stashed
in moldy breadbags or,
in a rusty lockbox,
ribbon-tied letters from a man
(a priest or married)
whose love words lay sour
years in her belly.
But no dice. Not even
a mean old cat
or its crumbling skull;
not much but dust
and empty spider webs,
and when we knocked those down,
nothing.

# Vandal

*What have you got,*
asks the stranger in town,
the Dangerous Man in denim

and leather, rubbing his bony
hip against your locker.
His work here

is already done,
you understand: you are
already torn to soft rags

and tied, red blurs
on the spokes of his wheels.
That mud on your chin

came off of his bootsoles;
those red strands of hair
between his teeth

are yours.
See how he cocks his neck,
how certain he is

that you will be demolished,
blue ribbon yanked
from your ponytail,

white oxford button-down ripped
against the seam.
Hooks from the stiff

white bra on the floor
of the janitor's closet,
pleated plaid skirt and white slip pushed up;

but he's already way down
the road from here;
he's already been gone years.

# What Brings You Tears?

*For Julie King*

Today on the road that brought me here,
to Med Check #3, the two dead dogs.

Yesterday, getting a letter that said
*Please don't call when Kate is here;*

*if you've something to say,*
*just write!* Stopped at red lights

I can well up recalling
cruel words delivered

twenty years ago.
*Christ, what the hell*

*are you crying about now?*
Tears for the kids

at the shelter, their chain-smoking
mothers stuffed into stained

polyester, threads popping
at puffy hips.

The dank smell of others'
bad choices and luck,

*other people's trouble,*
stings my eyes,

soothing the freshly raped girls
on the hotline, lungs drenched in menthol,

exhaling *Honey it's not your fault,*
*it's not* . . .

Or sometimes a song
reminds me of a man.

The first few chords might do it,
the place a soft drum

or piano breaks in, or the one perfect line
I know will come next,

to bomb out
my solar plexus.

So why turn it up then,
why the hell not turn it off?

*So what are you so
goddamn sad about this time,*

the mother and father
and lover want to know.

*I'll give you something
to cry about, young lady!*

So what brings you here today?
What brings these tears?

# Professor Love

Write about anything else in this world
but love, dear, he said;
now get off this junior high boy crazy shit
and get to it; write
about anything else but *love* and *loss*.

Besides which, what *love*
has one possibly *lost*
at your age, for chrissake, what are you,
22, 23? A baby! A puppy girl!

We ought to have coffee, he said,
I like that sweater.

I'll tell you about the work
of that ever-underrated
obscure-but-brilliant
abusive-but-misunderstood
bodybuilder/puppeteer/poet
I'm translating on a grant from the blah blah blah
or my doctoral days at Berkeley,
or my scandalous divorce from which I still
(as you've no doubt sensed)
have not fully recovered,
or why I can't find a good foreign film
or Thai restaurant, a halfway decent bottle of wine,
in this hick town, or grow a decent orchid
in my guest room this year.

So when are you coming for lunch?

That boy I saw you drinking with?
Not bright enough for you.
Write about anything else but him
and loving and losing boys like him;

as of this moment don't ever say *love*
or talk about loss in my class again;
now when
are we going to have dinner?

# Maiden Name

in seventy six or seven
 when some of us girls
  who got with the program
  were changing to wymin,
   changing our last names
    to cities or fruit
     not much got a chance
      to be funny anymore
       for instance
         when i said i want to be called
          chiquita banana
           after the girl with red red lips
            & a fruit bowl on top of her head
            doyle detroit (not her real name)
            called me a republican
fifteen odd years later
 when my love bug bit
   i got cornered in a hallway by a gal
    who introduced herself at parties as
     a radical-marxist-feminist-agent-of-change
      & she asked me now what's this i hear
       about you getting married & changing yr name
        taking on some man's name
         don't you know yr a role model
          at this university
           don't you know how many wymin
            fought for and fought in yr name
             don't you think you owe something
              back to the movement
hey where have i heard this voice before
i asked myself as i looked down & took the news
 from the RAD-MAR-FEM/AC
  all heated up in shame
   *such disappointing behavior young lady*
   *quite frankly we really expected better*
    *from you of all people*
     *to be blunt we are past appalled missy*

after that hallway shakedown
 i called that RAD-MAR-FEM/AC
  the marxist-with-a-mini-van
   behind her back
    was glad when her womanchild
     refused to wear overalls
      screamed her head off for frilly pink dresses
       my little ponies & malibu barbies
        all the way home from montessori school
but i know that gal was only
 doing her job
  how could she know
   how easily i
    zipped you down
     throat to toe
      *maiden name*
       stepped out of you new
        shook off the halves
         of hard shell
          carried thirty years
           how gladly i
            slipped you off
             my shoulders
              hung you back around
               my daddy's neck

# Missing

To watch you wave away
the ends of sentences
trailed off in dots,
those foldings and unfoldings
of your fingers, was more painful
than to witness
that ritual you made
of cracking every knuckle
the end of every day.

I'd have bitten every finger off
to please you, keep you near me,
under my succulent mouth
the thornteeth tucked
so deeply in my jaw.

And years and years now
no word. Send me a hook
or a noose or a case of razors
to cancel these regrets,
still young, in cages,

still howling the night
the doorbell sounds,
ice on the stairs
in the mold of your bootprint,

snow that might dust
your shoulders, your beard;
you back,
not one loose button,
not one frayed thread.

# Fourth of July

How do I tell a stranger the way,
as a girl,
I hoarded my unlit holiday loot
in a shoebox, and long
before dark on the Fourth of July
sneaked caps to hammer
out on the stoop,
fired lines of snaking carbon,
scattered my nickel sparks
as high as I could see?

Half a woman saved since then
for someone or other: mouth,
a pair of arms, a working brain,
a sheet of skin.
Smiling face lit up in wait
for someone or other
who'd *come to his senses*
soon enough, someone or other
*on the horizon*, or
just up the road, who'd find her,
his arms full of roses, roses . . .

The wine in my veins runs cool.
The fireflies blink.
Our language stops.
The kind moon is a stone.
Kiss me: the weeds
are taller than our faces.

# Cleanup

*For Joseph Gemin*

Brown apple cores float
in half glasses of Guinness
next to your stacks of cards
full of cryptic notes,
improbable plots and charts
and deep-bitten pencils, the wreck
of your late night brooding
left for me. And I am as proud
of your clutter as I am resentful,
the only way I can be wifely.

But hail to those whose daily bread
depends upon our messes:
the highway crew scraping
the crumpled fawn, her bloodstuck fur,
from the melting tar;
the high school custodian,
dustpan full of butts,
wringing prom vomit out of his mop;
our mothers, their mothers, and on up the line,
hands bone raw from bleaching diapers,
scouring toilets, scrubbing walls.

Not to mention the rubbish
too heavy to haul,
overflowing the file drawers
and hard drives of surgeons and lawyers,
senators, shrinks, and environmental engineers,
the white-collar cleanup crew we pay
to carry our stench,
to sort through and disinfect
our daily rubble.

After you, without whom
my own snarls would have never come smooth,

I will always clean up.
But never forget the resolve it takes
to wade through another's mud,
another's refuse;
the rugged love,
the industrial strength.

# Upper Peninsula Landscape with Aunts

Home from casino or fish fry,
the aunts recline
in their sisters' dens,
kicking off canvas shoes
and tucking their nylon footies
inside, remarking
on each others' pointy toes
and freckled bunions.

When Action 2 News comes on
they shake their heads and *tsk tsk tsk*
and stroke their collarbones.
The aunts hold their shoulderstrap purses
tight into their hips
and doublecheck their back seats.
The last politician they trusted
was FDR, and only then
when he kept his pants on.

The aunts won't be dickered down,
they'll tell you *a buck is a buck,*
as they wash and rinse freezer bags,
scrape off aluminum foil.

The aunts know exciting ways
with government cheese,
have furnished trailer homes
with S&H green stamp lamps and Goodwill sofas;
brook trout and venison thaw
in their shining sinks.

With their mops and feather dusters
and buckets of paint on sale,
with their hot glue guns and staplers
and *friendly plastic* jewelry kits,

with their gallons of closeout furniture stripper,
the aunts are hurricanes who'll marbleize
the inside of your closets
before you've had time
to put coffee on.

The aunts are steam-powered, engine-driven,
early rising women of legendary
soap and water beauty
who've pushed dozens of screaming babies
out into this stolen land.
They take lip or guff from no man,
child, or woman; tangle with aunts
and they'll give you what for times six
and then some: don't *make* them come up those stairs!

And yes they are acquainted
with the Bogeyman,
his belly full of robbery and lies.
The aunts have aimed deer rifles
right between his eyes, dead-bolted him out
and set their dogs upon him,
or gone tavern to tavern to bring him home,
carried him down from his nightmare
with strong black tea, iced his split lips,
painted his fighting cuts with Mercurochrome.

And they have married Cornishmen and Swedes,
and other Irish, married their sons and daughters off
to Italians and French and Finlanders;
buried their parents and husbands and each other,
buried their drowned and fevered and miscarried children;
turned grandchildren upside down
and shaken the swallowed coins loose
from their windpipes; ridden the whole wide world
on the shelves of their hips.

The aunts know paradise is born
from rows of red dirt, red coffee cans,
prayers for rain. Whenever you leave
their houses, you leave with pockets and totes
full of strawberry jam and rum butter balls
and stories that weave themselves into your hair.

Some have already gone to the sky
to make pasties and reorganize the cupboards.
The rest will lead camels
through needles' eyes
to the shimmering kingdom of Heaven.

# FOUR

# Toyland

# Venice

I've been there: 1989. Ate squid and scampi
with the heads on, and made crazy love there too,

with a man who loved me, in a pink hotel with a back
garden swing and all the little green birds singing.

The whole country smells like dark coffee brewing, strong
as ground black rock and as fresh in your mind

as the twists and rolls of bread and narrow streets
and hills and lovemaking, and even in the tiniest cafés

bowls and bowls of yellow bell-shaped flowers float,
and clusters of lilies the color of lavender cream;

and in evening the smoky dark olive girls
stroll arm in arm and smile *Buona séra, Signóra,* because

you are the nice American lady. But it's more the Venetian colors
that seep through your pores, crawl

into your blood – the wind-washed golds and rusty reds
and greens rubbed in terra cotta, flung upon hillsides

and stacked up along canals – mouth-watering colors
recalling the tastes of olives and cheese and wine;

so years later, when you're driving back home, north
on Highway 141 past Pembine Pawn & Gun, and see

those four boxcars out in the waving grass and chicory weed,
boxcars stained wind-washed gold and rusty red and green

rubbed in terra cotta, you've got it all back: pink stucco hotel
with green birds singing, yellow bellflowers, lavender cream,

strong coffee, smoky girls and cheese, scampi and rivers of
wine and crazy in love in Venice, in springtime, in 1989.

# Tarzania

Run down the weeded hill
from your screen door to the train tracks;

brush away milkweed, snakeweed, chokeweed;
push up your skirt, put your knees

right down into the gravel, and lay
your ear flat on the cool rail

just like the Indians did. Drink
the low thunder down into your throat,

let it flood through your lungs, and keep
your eyes closed till you catch

the first whiff of train clouds puffing
out over the red bridge rail.

Now get up and peel the stones from your knees
and back off from the tracks like you promised

your mother, stand up and back off
a way up the hill, and get ready

to throw your arms out and over your head
and then jump, jump; whistle roar coming

right up through your shoe soles
even as they leave Earth; and then do it:

go on and scream just as long and as loud as you can,
TARZANIA, GIRL QUEEN of the Metro Jungle.

# X-Ray Tech

Shayla's my daughter's age if I had one,
not neat as I'd like her, but nice
enough, in her Green Bay Packers
sweatshirt on dress-down Friday
at the Breast Clinic, green & gold
helmets bouncing off her ears
as she points me into the dressing room.
Needitalloffontop, she says, meaning
sweater and bra and then tying the much-laundered
gown with blue snowflakes in back,
and I wink and say Go Pack Go.
Shayla's too young to remember
the x-ray vans up from Detroit
to our Kmart *Plaza*, lines of itchy kids
in Red Ball Jets strung out to Electric Ave.
all waiting to see our skeletons on a screen
while our mothers, done up
in rollers and bumpy scarves and pink lipstick,
cruised the aisles for everyday low,
low prices.
It wasn't a lump we were looking for then, but proof
that our science books were right: under skin
we were really as scary as Halloween, hung
in a spooky dance from skull to metatarsal,
loose and connected at once, and ready
to snap off that long stem of spine
anywhere, anytime.
And we knew it wasn't a funhouse
fake, this machine that could see inside us, see
spots of red devils popping along our bones
when *cancer* was still a phantom in the neighborhood,
when an out-of-town man in a lab jacket flipped a switch
and our luminous neon grins lit the darkness, wide
and white-hot in that tiny world.

# The Visible Man

For Christmas, he got me the microscope:
    his girl
would be up in her room observing
the glorious liquid world
in a drop of saliva,
    his girl
would be little Miss Leeuwenhoek,
counting germs swimming backstroke
on slides,
    while other girls
counted jumprope skips, threw fistfuls
of silver jacks.

Then for my birthday: THE VISIBLE MAN,
that wacky assortment
of pop-in, pop-out boy parts
in a box,
whose see-through snap-together halves
left him no secrets.

While Barbie and Midge
and the other girl dolls
ran screaming from him on tippy toes,
I heard him say
    *Get used to it sweethearts,*
    *with this guy what you see*
    *is what you get.*

While other girls dreamed of boys
who'd come already perfect
to save them,
in cowboy hats, on perfect plastic horses,
    his girl would be busy
building her own,
    seeing his heart
stayed in the right place,
    seeing his brain
stayed up in his skull,
    paving the shortest way
to his shining soul.

# Hans Brinker Was My Boyfriend

Those were the days, Hans;
when your father was still
a *dunderdunk,* dead in the head
from a bump on the dikes

and you and your mom and Gretel
still lived in that ratty cottage
on the wrong side of the canal –
when you needed me, Hans.

I was the one who waited rinkside,
rocking blade to blade, freezing
my little rear end off under my tights
while you whittled your wooden skates;

not Hilda, not Katrinka – it was me, Hans,
with chattering teeth,
feeling dumb in my fur-trimmed muff
and my red flannel skirt from Amsterdam,

the appliqué ribbon trailing
delightfully down from my hips,
in case you didn't notice, Hans.
In case you forgot.

And yet in that spring of '66,
just weeks before the flood,
when you clomped up the walk to my door,
your blonde hair falling

all over your forehead
past your pale eyebrows
and into your eyes,
your arms full of yellow tulips,

I could not speak . . .

Those were the days, Hans,
before the big race,
before you found the nerve
to find that famous doctor

whose sharp and gleaming instruments
would make your daddy sit up,
thump his skull, and remember
the family fortune was under the stump,

cold cash for the woolens
and wines and rich red meat
Dame Brinker and the kids
had ten years been without.

Not that I wasn't thrilled for you, Hans,
but that was the end of us.
I hear you're a doctor yourself now,
in Amsterdam.

You should know: I still skate in my dreams,
in stocking feet,
through shopping malls and halls
of my old schools,

and fast, Hans, fast,
my dreamy head bent low,
that smell of fresh-slashed ice
alive and dancing in my lungs.

And when I come out of my dizzy spins,
you're there to catch me; out of
my figure eights I snowplow
into your wonderful arms.

We live in a house on the Zuider Zee,
our windmill and built-in pool
in back, our beds full of ripe Dutch bulbs
and little Brinkers.

A thousand guilders in the bank,
we light the stove, we stay in love,
we glide through our diamond days
on skates of silver.

# Toyland

Midnight exactly my momma snores,
and daddy pokes her thigh.
Through the wall I hear them
patting back the pillows,
rustling in the quilts,
and the minute they fall back
I'm bound for Toyland,
rocked out of my maple four-poster
and ready to roll.

Untouchable Japanese princess dolls
steam out of their crystal domes,
pry themselves out of their half-hoof shoes,
shake back their kimonos,
jump down from the dresser top,
bone combs whipped
from their long black hair.

Then Midge and the girls
sneak out of the Dream House windows,
careful in heels and prom dresses,
in bunnyfur wraps, in high bouffants;
and Anita, the pink-haired walking doll,
winks by the window, wand gleaming, tiara on fire.

> We touch but her pink net skirt
> and we are upheld . . .

Out of the window
we fly like geese
over Schwanagers' rooftop,
the ice rink, the root beer stand;
then hanging a louie out over the tracks,
waving down to the bums hiking drunk.
Over the drive-in movie,
the bean docks, the freighters,
the chemical smokestacks;

over the bridge lit up to Canadaland –
hey Canada, eat our dust!

In Toyland the streets
are candystick twists;
we groove in that lemon-lime town
where the fun never stops, and the hits
just keep on coming.

We jump to the Freddy,
hop to the pony, get hep
with the Watusi, too.
And when Tressy lets her hair down
we all stand back: nobody can do
the shingaling like she do.

Skipper and Ken do the limbo rock,
Barb tilts the stick lower and lower,
and even the Bride Doll offs her veil
to frug with the Visible Man
just one more time before Her Day.

And I'm the tallest
living doll around.

In this town they call me *Belinda,*
better known as Queen of Bugaloo.
Yeah, I'm out without permission,
barefoot and in my pj's,
what about it?
This is Toyland. I'm Belinda. I'm the babe.

# Down There

In the days before maples
sent spinners too early,
when you could still pop
green maple-spun wishbones,
get juice in your eyes,

the thickening wail of an ambulance
streamed down 10th from St. Catherine's
right up my street to my curb
full of chestnut blossoms,
right up to my house on Electric Ave.

Mrs. "Four Walls & Five Kids" Tingle,
the cow next door, used to roll her eyes
when us neighborhood Mackerel Snapper kids
made our signs of the cross for St. Cat's sirens,
but not this time.

Outside in her greasy pink housecoat
and pink sponge curlers, she choked up
when my ma came out on the stretcher,
her fuschia-caked mouth a round O,
until everyone cleared
and went home to their kitchens
to whip up a hot dish for me and my dad.

*Looks like now*
*you're an only child for sure,* she clucked,
lighting another filterless Lucky,
*your ma's gone and ruptured herself*
*down there. She's ripped her womb,*
*she's lost her woman-ness.*

*Rupture:* I saw an inky red wound
spread tentacle legs, fan wide.
*Womb:* I saw a soft-boiled egg
float free and loose; a soft-shelled
hatchling bouncing

off bruise-purple walls, the sister
I'd been praying for.

*Embryo, uterus, ovary:* all creatures of a world
my mother carried with her effortlessly,
everywhere she went, all sloshing
wall to wall with each wide salty swing
of her generous hips; her warm water ocean belly
a regular seaworld with tides of its own;
a dancing aquarium full of friendly starfish,
sand dollars, seahorse sperm.

And for you, Joyce Tingle, I saw
a heat-conducting metal folding chair
reserved down there,
in the basement of Southern Purgatory.

I saw the Pope scratch your name
off the Master Prayer List,
caught a whiff of your spongies sizzling,
imagined the balls of your crumpled
toes curling to toast,
tapping away on the red hot ceiling of Hell.

# Senior Picture, 1971

I take it all back,
each dirty, lowdown thing I ever said
and felt and thought about you, honey,
and all I put you through.

I take back your Clearasil zits and Midol cramps,
take back those cheap four-inch gold-plated hoops
that infected your earlobes
and snagged your silk shirts;
I take it all back to the Kmart for you,
stand in the returns line
with armfuls of too-tight bras, blue eyeshadows,
Uncurl and water weight pills.

I take back the menthol stink of those nasty
fags you smoked, breathe in the foul clouds
you blew out your bedroom window;
take out the butts you double-wrapped
in Kleenex, sprayed with Glade,
snuck out to the backyard trash can;

take back the pink frosted lipstick
and jasmine cologne you stole from Hudson's,
take back the drive-in nights
you puked popcorn and apple wine
out the windows of fast-moving cars,
take back your dancing wild at the Bowl-O-Drome;

your animal, rabid fear of touching
and being touched; your fear of boylust burning
bright as a thousand votives
in St. Joseph's vestibule;
fear of the Lone Airborne Sperm,
fear of the Lord's cool hand
set down hard upon your backside,
fear of His crown of thorns
set down hard upon your hairdo;

take back your venial sins chalked up in fives
on your blank slate soul.

I take back your fear of fat, stronger
than your fear of God, the fear
that kept saying *no thank you,*
*none for me, please;* that whittled you down and down
with your chocolate milk lunches
from 116 to 106 to 96 pounds
that Easter you went to Florida;

and even with studio-tinted cheeks
and hair the photographer made too red,
naturally wavy hair set straight
on juice cans and Dippity-Doo the night before;
and even in spite of that goofy far-off someday look
that picture pulled out of your face
from God knows where,

I can see it so crystal
clearly now, decades too late,
see your momma was all along right
about you:
you were one sweet bird,
one inside/outside beautiful
special girl.

# Bombshelter

*The bomb could explode any time of the year, day or night,*
*Sundays, holidays, vacation time — we must be ready every*
*day, all the time, to do the right thing if the atomic bomb*
*explodes . . . it's a bomb! Duck! And cover!*
— Children's Civil Defense Instruction Film, circa 1960

First, the megaton flashbulb, stronger
than sixteen million brownie cameras
going off at once. And then the astonishing,
fabulous blast, and the massive red fireball mushrooms
with hurricane stems, and then
it's goodbye Jesus, so long Christmas,
hello pledge allegiance to Nikita
year-round, seven days a week,
droning the Volga boat song
in scratchy red uniforms
under the hammer and sickle,
zombie brains washed clean
with twenty mule team Borax, every stain
of Catechism bleached away, and nothing
but boiled root vegetables to chew on.

*Bury us, my ass,* my father said to the TV,
dying for a Chesterfield,
*bloody beetmonger bully! Shoe-pounding Commie dwarf!*
But damned if our neighbor Bill Tingle
wasn't out on weekends
laying brick for a seven-man bombshelter
the other side of the lilacs
just past our clothesline;
and damned if his wife Joyce
wasn't trotting home from the A&P
stocked up on Campbell's and saltines,
Pet milk and canned potatoes.

*And damned if the whole bloody family*
*ain't out there in the spectacle!* dad said,
chomping a wad of Beeman's, dying for a Chesterfield,
as Tingle kids bagged wagonfuls of sand.

*First all the water's poison,*
then all the hamburger, then your skin peels off,
and then you're just a skeleton,
Bunny Tingle told me,
but her dad said he'd rather be peeled alive
than turn into a Commie.

*Joyce says they're going to have ping pong in there,*
my mom said, *can you imagine?*
Fourteen hundred bricks,
eight hundred feet of steel reinforcing,
asphalt shingles, baffle walls, sixty pounds of nails
and a ping pong table. *Joyce says her husband says*
*those Cubans aren't kidding!*

Those nights, as the bricks next door climbed higher
and higher, rose into a roof,
I dreamt of rivers red with poison,
five great boiling lakes, water on fire
in our basement pipes, and woke with my mouth
wide open. What if the Tingles
won't give us a drink of their water?
What if the A-bomb goes off and the Tingles
won't let us in? What if we pound and pound
and the Tingles just keep right on
playing ping pong?

*Then we'll huff and we'll puff and we'll*
*blow their bombshelter down,* mom told me.

*Then it's me and Bill Tingle's fight to the finish*
*out under the apple trees with pointed sticks,*
my dad said, lighting another Chesterfield.

My dad versus Bunny's dad.
As the sky rattled out of its cage.
As our giant bluebird world flew off
through mushroom clouds,
to someplace we couldn't name.

# O Bernadette

*Bernadette has the childlike quality of visualizing the spoken word. To her no phrases are empty.*
— Franz Werfel, *The Song of Bernadette*

Show me, Bernadette,
I will believe you.

I want to see what you saw
in the grotto,
crossing the stream
for your bundle
of kindling sticks.

Show me the Virgin's bare feet,
the stems of yellow roses
between her toes,
the crescent moons
of her perfect toenails
here in the wallpaper pattern;
show me her egg-blue sash.

Let all of my staring
come to something good;
deliver me signed
and sealed in grace,
arrived in faith like rain.

Make me as you were,
poor and plain
but certain;
small, dark, and lovely
in my one clean dress.

A true Midwesterner, PAMELA GEMIN was born in Ann Arbor, Michigan, in 1954, and has lived in Wisconsin since 1983. Her poems have appeared in many literary journals across the country, and she is coeditor of *Boomer Girls: Poems by Women from the Baby Boom Generation,* an anthology of women's coming-of-age poetry published by the University of Iowa Press. Besides her current job teaching composition, literature, and creative writing at the University of Wisconsin Oshkosh, Gemin teaches workshops in creative writing for adults as well as middle school and high school students. Gemin is currently enrolled in the MFA in Writing Program at Vermont College, and lives with her husband, Joseph, in Oshkosh, Wisconsin.